Ho Him Go Wild With Pleasure In Bed:

Easy and Quick Ways To Please Him That Will Have Him Beg You For More!

VERONICA SUMMERS

This page left intentionally blank.

CONTENTS

1 INTRODUCTION

This book is meant to serve as a guide for women on how to get a man to untold heights of passion while helping set free his tamed secret desires in bed.

As a woman, no doubt you know a romantic guy from right at the very moment you land your eyes on him. Even when you're only dating him and you two are yet to sample the sack together, there is the way he blinks at you, touches your face, kisses you, holds or caresses you that tells you he is a die-hard romantic.

Just because people claim women are needy, it does not necessarily mean that they should be considered the weaker gender; at least not when it comes to romance and sex. In fact, there is nothing as liberating as a woman who knows her way around the bedroom and who isn't scared to initiate lovemaking.

Given the idea that it isn't necessarily to give him a hard-on but to keep him on that sexual high, you would need to do more than just a good blow to top the list. It becomes solely you he wants and desires, regardless of how many half-dressed women he meets on the street. The goal is to leave an impression on him such that he has you in his mind wherever he goes, whatever he does.

In essence, when it comes to your man, no loving should ever be better than yours unless, of course, you are ready to share him. So the need becomes definite to not just excite him behind closed doors but to also stimulate him to such heights of passion that he only fantasizes on both, in terms of talk and action.

While you cannot afford to be a trophy girl for him, continue reading this guide and hopefully the tips are not just able to help you drive your man wild with pleasure in bed but to also evoke in him the feeling of the 'luckiest man ever,' resulting in him staying with you; this is the idea- so let's gets started!

2 CARRYING THE RIGHT ATTITUDE

Be Sex-Positive

Interestingly, sex for women starts in the mind and, like it or not, what you feed your mind during sex dictates whether you end up having a great time or just participating in the act.

Being sex-positive means having a state of mind that facilitates a healthier, more positive and happier view of sex in general. Being sex-positive further means that you are aware that it is okay to feel inclined to have sex and that you need not feel any sort of guilt.

If you have ever felt the need to apologize for being a sexual being, erase that thought. Rather, think of how incredibly good sex can enhance your self-esteem and lifestyle too.

Don't Just Lie There

It's sad to think that for most people, it is during sex that they start building castles and anticipating the future. You know, like you are just lying there thinking of what you need to get from the grocery store later on or where your kids are going to start school.

Practically, what happens during sex depends on the attitude you bring with you. For ladies especially, if you decide to wait until you feel in the mood for sex, you can bet you will be waiting for an extremely long time. You see, when parenthood sets in, as your career becomes demanding and as you quickly approach menopause, it is hard to rely on your body to set the pace for sex.

Thankfully, women's sex drives lie entirely in their minds. So, if you decide tonight is the night that I am going to explore the heights of passion, your body will tune in too. However, as a call for action, you might really need to stop lying there during sex and start paying some attention to your body. Know what feels goods, how you want to be touched, what takes you a notch higher.

Instead of wondering how long it is going to take you to participate in sex with your partner, start enjoying the moment by letting the feeling of arousal and orgasm serve as unmonitored revitalization.

Just Let It Happen

You can't force sex upon your relationship; good sex must be allowed to thrive. In fact, pursuing orgasm brings about performance anxiety, which, as a result, undermines sexual arousal. You see, the reason most people end up faking orgasms is because they are trying too hard to make it work. If anything, relax and simply enjoy the moment.

Allow yourself to explore sex and the pleasures formed within it. This means you need to stop judging yourself, feeling self-conscious or guilty or dwelling in personal hang-ups. Again, that to-do list can wait, as you need to invest utmost dedication during sex to fully enjoy the moment.

Pursue Self-Validation

Instead of worrying every minute-*every second even*, about how you are doing in bed, start validating yourself as good enough. Never, ever place your self-esteem or self-worth at other people's mercy. When you approach sex with this positive attitude, saying to yourself, 'I am really good in this' instead of 'I am awful in bed,' you change everything else that follows.

Men want to have sex with someone who is not there for the sake of it, but that can allow themselves to be actually into it and present in the moment. It is likely that you view letting him pursue and conquer you as giving him a precious and divine gift, but sadly he may not acknowledge that fact as intensely as you would want him to.

So what happens? You need to stop participating in sex as some sort of favor to him or using it as bait while expecting something in return as that is a major turn-off for men. In essence, a guy wants to be with a woman who enjoys the moment just as much as him.

Dealing With Frustrations

You see that you are going to retain a positive mindset when it comes to sex, and it won't be because you don't suffer daily frustrations or experience knock-down fights, but because you choose to focus on what remains when all is said and done.

Do you love him so much that you would do anything for him? Well, how about making the resolution of never transiting daily stresses and frustrations to your bedroom and instead, allowing it to be your sanctuary for healing and relaxation.

The feelings provoked by your time alone with him in the bedroom should be able to provoke this warm and fuzzy glow and not bring tension. Maintaining a positive sexual attitude remains a proactive move towards a fulfilled sex life.

3 INITIATING ROMANCE

Come Out of the Shell

There is no doubt that the thought of transitioning to being a sexual woman can deem quite terrifying and intimidating. However, truth be told, most women still remain trapped in their sexual shell, desperate for liberation. They look forward to a time they can be sexually uninhibited, relaxed and free to express their sexuality without the worry of being judged.

In fact, most women worry that if they become sexually liberated and free, men will view this approach as 'trashy' or as 'too willing'. No woman wants to be seen as needy, especially when it comes to sex. However, what most women do not know is that relentless counts of holding back on genuine passion for fear of being judged eventually translates as unwillingness to being more sexually adventurous with their men.

So you see, while you are sitting there worrying that he might judge you for being sexually liberated, what you do not realize is that he is there scared of proposing a more passionate approach to sex. Better sex ensues when we decide to get out of our 'sexual shell' in pursuit for the utmost satisfaction.

Again, no man ever got turned on by a woman wearing a miserable bathrobe or pajamas. Take the initiative to feel sexy: go shopping for something sexy and pretty!

With immense options in the lingerie department, such as lace-topped stockings and pretty nightgowns, you have no more reason to keep making lame excuses as to why you cannot find an outfit that stays true to your style all-the-while igniting interest in the bedroom. It must be in due time to claim your sexual freedom, but remember that getting out of the shell also means taking the initiative to initiate sex on occasion.

So Who Initiates Romance or Sex?

Another grave misconception that most people have had long enough is thinking that it is quite normal for men to initiate romance and sex. It is true that men always come off as sexy and romantic when being in charge during sex; it is also true that men do not need to be wanted or desired to ignite their sexual drive, but they certainly appreciate it when they are needed, desired, wanted and admired without reason.

As we said earlier, what happens during sex for women is completely dependent on their attitude. So after you have climbed out of your sexual shell and are feeling all sexy, don't be shy to initiate sex! You don't get bonus points for pretending to be submissive, coy or for acting shy. How about changing the odds tonight and giving your lovemaking a major head-start?

Where is Your Sexual Energy?

Let's say you were brought up to being demure, the 'good girl' type. In this case, you may find it really hard to openly express and explore your feminine elements during sex. This approach might have been a bonus point while you were still single, but the same move is immensely suicidal when in a sexual relationship.

The lack of sexual energy might as easily be translated as unwillingness or reluctance towards sex. Men want an active partner, that is willing and able to make noises and thrust and not simply wait upon him to dictate what happens during sex; this is key.

Believe it or not, men anticipate the day that you are able to express your uninhibited passion during sex. Whether it means going on top with him unalarmed, positioning yourself in the best way that brings the greatest pleasure, being unafraid to kiss him passionately or being assertive with what you want during sex.

How to Initiate Sex

You have most definitely acquainted yourself with the huge benefits that come with having good sex. With the art of holding enough ground to helping improve your health and boosting your sleep, the bonus benefit is that sex helps strengthen relationships. Think therefore of the decision to initiate sex as a bonus step towards strengthening your relationship.

So it becomes quite apparent that the best way to have more sex is to be able to ask for it. While it may not be as easy to get this message across given such external culprits as exhaustion, shyness and fear, here are some tips on how you can initiate sex with your man.

Establish a 'Sex Code'

Given that all the words in the dictionary were once invented, why not just invent one yourself and use it to communicate a 'call for sex' to your partner? Keep in mind that it should be something that you are comfortable saying in front of friends, kids and relatives.

While the designated 'secret code' you choose may sound ordinary to everyone else, how it stirs up intimacy and excitement between you and your partner will become the punch line. It can be as simple as these phrases 'Honey, are we making cupcakes later?" or "Babe, this headache is killing me!" Whatever statement or reference code you choose as your 'I'm in the mood' code, allow it to work wonders for your sex life!

Getting in the Mood

When you wish to summon sex, don't just get in the mood as this will only remain a battle half-won. Instead, take the initiative to stay in the mood. You may not fancy reading, but a romantic paragraph in a romance novel or a grasp of sensual images puts you right into that sexual state. However, while this may still not necessarily work for you, you can try reminiscing on the last time you had sex with him; this should definitely help revamp that sexual appetite.

Non-Verbal Cues

Could it be that verbal requests for sex are not within your comfort zone? In such case, try a non-verbal gesture. Something like ear-nibbling while he is watching TV, kissing his neck or stroking his arm when seated next to him may work better for you. These gestures not only catch him by surprise but also highly boosts sexual feelings, and in response, some spontaneous sex too.

Generous Complements

Noticing and respectively acknowledging positive attributes in him works incredibly well, especially if the complements are made while in the bedroom. This not only fosters affection, but also works as indirect seduction.

Something like "Honey, you always look so sexy while in the kitchen cooking me dinner" or "You know what hun, you always look so hot in those shorts mowing our lawn." There is no limit to the sensations such complements in the bedroom can arouse.

Change the Norm

Often in relationships, there happen to be a time indirectly designated for sex, like after tucking the kids into bed, washing and putting away the dishes, or ironing; in essence, after you are done with the day chores. However, the best timing is when there is no timing at all. Consider changing from the ordinary and try surprising him when he least expects it.

Maybe he is in the kitchen and you just walk right behind him hugging him from behind, teasing about a time you once had sex in the kitchen. When you walk up to a man with a horny attitude that says you want to do it right now, right here, then that is all the motivation he needs to bang you right there, right then. Nothing feels good like off-guard sex: unplanned, unmonitored and definitely uncensored.

4 THE POWER OF SEDUCTION

Get and Keep his Attention

You see, as a woman, when you set your eyes on a man you want to have for keeps, you will do everything to keep him. There is nothing as sexually intense as being able to make him putty in your hands.

For men, it is no-brainer that sight is their most active sense. Their sexual hyperactivity is mostly compelled by the sense of sight with other senses following along complementarily.

How You Dress

Given that men are visual beings, you should know that they look out for a visually stimulating sight. Someone that dresses flirtatiously and sexy and, this goes without saying, that you must dress for sexual success.

The idea, however, is not to come off as a slut with too much make up, blubbery or carrying a slutty outlook. It is about being sensual and sexy, graceful and confident, persuasive and irresistible, all at the same time.

Mental Seduction

Seduce a man physically and he will be yours for the night but seduce him mentally and he will be yours forever. You see, when it comes to seduction, it should be less about the physical aspect and much more about the mental.

Have you never encountered a guy who would have gotten all of the pretty girls completely slayed, yet he was not your definition of hot or even attractive? This is how seduction works; it is a lot more mental than physical.

Body Language

You should know that nothing is as intoxicating as confidence in a woman. Being shy will rarely get the guy you want hooked. On the contrary, you will find that your lack of confidence only attracts weak guys, those especially intimidated by a woman with a mind of her own. While pursuing the art of seduction, you are no doubt pursuing the title of a sexual goddess.

Know that you will only achieve this if you let your body do the talking. When you lick your lips subtly while uttering something sensual, you are communicating your kissing skills. Gently touching sensual parts of your body says you know how to get things going.

You cannot afford to get upset because his first interest is your body; he is a guy and a primitive creature. Instead, why not acknowledge this aspect and let it work out to your advantage? So it is your body he wants, let him have it but play close attention to how you carry yourself; even without sex talk, you leave an irresistible impression.

How to Seduce Him

Successful seduction with your man not only helps strengthen your relationship, but it also heats up the bedroom mood too. While sex remains beneficial and a necessity, we often overlook this key aspect; here is how to achieve faultless seduction:-

1. Tease him both with what he can and cannot have. For example, when you walk into the shower right after him and know he will just have to bang you or bang you!

2. Dirty talk- Hello! It is a part of liberation when you communicate exactly what you want. You are hot for him and you want him right there and then- let him know.

3. Direct talk- Sometimes you just want him to skip foreplay and just rough it up deep

and fierce with a quickie, it's okay to lead him on.

4. Thinking of a new sex position? Perfect! Say you have always wanted to try out a certain position or just came across it in a lifestyle magazine, initiate it!

5. Do not expect him to read your mind. You know your G-spot too well, so take his hand and lead him there. Show him how and where you want to be touched, let him explore you.

6. Maybe he is busy doing his daily reports or watching his favorite game? Start touching yourself in front of him and don't hold back on masturbating while biting your lip. He will know you mean business and will be undressing you in no time.

7. Go panty-less in the bedroom. After a relaxing shower just throw on his baggy t-shirt and ditch your panties. Then just as if you are not aware of it, bend over at the drawer and pretend you are looking for something. The sight of a woman's vagina from behind is incredibly wooing to a man!

8. While getting ready for work, stroll around the room with nothing but your panties, bra and heels. Girl, you leave him no option but to make you his!

9. Wake up before him. He is still asleep; brush your boobs against his back, pretending you are unaware of the possible effect. You wake him up and with a mighty hard-on!

He is busy with his dinner after a hard day's work: slowly remove your panties, making sure he can see you, and then throw them on his lap or hand them to him before walking to the bedroom. How he follows without a word, even he cannot explain it.

5 MAXIMIZING ON FOREPLAY

Men and Foreplay

Often times, emphasis is endured more on how much foreplay matters to women, but then again, men's sexual drive also highly benefits from foreplay. While foreplay helps maintain the heights of intimacy both physically and emotionally, men highly reap from foreplay because it means more prolonged and longer sexual episodes.

So while being able to prolong foreplay is not only beneficial to your man, but to you too, sometimes men form the fear of losing an erection and tend to possess this fear of sexual foreplay. This fear drives them to rush into intercourse while skipping or cutting short foreplay.

What you Can Do

It is really ironic that guys work so hard to maintain an erection, while if women were to be asked, a longer erection is never the cutting edge for them.

So he is downright worried of subjecting you to a moment of sexual disappointment in case he loses an erection after too much foreplay. In this case, you realize that he is too afraid of his sexual performance being judged on the longevity of his erection. Communicate what matters most to you. That it is in how he pleases you during foreplay that counts and not necessarily how long he can thrust it up; he needs to know that.

When you do not communicate your preferences and needs, your man ends up thinking his short-lived erection is a downer and probably turns to Viagra. That not only breeds sexual insecurity for him, but also leaves the both of you still missing on the utmost satisfaction.

However, if he knows that it is not the length of his erection that counts but the length of the foreplay, then the two of you will work around the odds to help blow each other's mind with indescribable pleasure.

Foreplay and a Longer Erection

During sexual arousal, the woman's muscles contract, making more room in her vagina and, no doubt, this makes sex more comfortable and pleasurable.

A man wants to have sex with a woman who is comfortable with him inside of her and the slightest onset of fake sexual pleasure becomes a psychological turn-off. Again, foreplay helps to boost a woman's lubrication from the excitement and arousal, which, in turn, helps to get a man erect and respectively, maintain an erection.

A man struggles less with attaining an orgasm if foreplay had been maximized before intercourse.

Foreplay Tips and Tricks

Guys love foreplay especially when it's done right so you need not question how much they enjoy it. By knowing how to tease him right, pursuing foreplay with your man will see you enjoying sex a lot more than you did before.

Maybe earlier on in your relationship all he needed was to see your naked body to get a hard-on, but as time elapses, things get too obvious and repetitive. In essence, with time, you can no longer deny that the novelty is no more; this is when you need to start focusing more on his mind than his sense of sight to keep him hyper in bed. Here are some compelling foreplay tips and tricks that will work magic for your sex life.

Go Grinding

This means erotic movements using your butt against his thighs and his penis area. When the mood is already set for sex, his mind is already focused on touching you and some deep penetration. Change the odds by making some rules tonight. Ask him to keep his hands off of your body completely and if anything, you are only allowed to touch him.

Start grinding on him, which will instantly prompt a serious hard-on. Not only will he have a clear, intoxicating sight of your clitoris as you work your body on him, but you also get to stimulate your pubic area too.

Keep this up with alternative strokes and kisses before you finally blow the whistle and tell him that he is now free to touch you. Believe me when I tell you that he won't be touching you at all but grabbing you so hard that his mind and sexual energy is optimized for a payback session. You can expect rough, deep and mind blowing penetration and ecstatic orgasms on both ends.

Get Your Hands to Work

While kissing is often used to initiate foreplay, try incorporating other techniques like touching and massaging him with your hands.

Go for his most sensitive parts like the inner thighs, ears, neck, cheeks and the back of his head, caressing him softly and gently so that it feels ticklish and sensual.

Tongue his Penis

To achieve fiery foreplay, incorporate cold and hot sensations on him. Ice works just perfect when put in your mouth so your tongue is ice-cold before you give him an icy tongue swirl on the tip of his penis. Not only is this move mind-blowing, but the transition from a warm frenzy to an ice-cold sensation helps prolong his erection too.

Provocative Oral Sex

So he is often the one to go 'down there,' licking every part of you and damn! You know how heavenly it feels. Why not try returning the favor by teasing his body senseless?

Get on your knees while provocatively maintaining eye contact, start licking his inner thighs through soft, long, unmonitored strokes all the while alternating these with gentle kisses. Make sure to delay licking his goodies; lick them after exploring his inner thighs, abdomen and chest area.

Sharing a Bath or Shower

Nothing brings a couple closer better than sharing a bath together, especially after a long day of work. Make sure to enjoy and relax in his arms in the beginning without immediately focusing on sex.

Playing with his body underneath the warm sensations of a bubble bath will get him so hot for you that you might never even make it to the bedroom.

Touching Yourself

It doesn't even necessarily have to be masturbation in the bedroom, but if you start touching your body gently while still dressed up, you cannot imagine the vibrations you arouse.

After you get him drawn to you, you can start complaining of a sore muscle, a move that will prompt him to offer you a massage and you can bet his mind is already turned on for you.

6 GET NAUGHTY & BE CONFIDENT AT IT

Dare to Break the Rules

Sometimes to be able to spice things up in the bedroom, it will mean that you have an open-minded approach to sex, such that you don't hold back on anything.

If only you had the chance to tap in on men's dark secrets, you would be awed at the magnitude of things they wished their women would try on them. A guy who has been lucky enough to be with a bad girl knows how legendary they come off.

Just because you are not like that vixen in that erotic novel doesn't mean you cannot still measure up! Are you asking yourself why you should go to the trouble? Men love it when you carry a fearless, uninhibited attitude to the bedroom.

They like when you are able to break the rules, cross your set boundaries and ask for what you want without a fleet. Yes, that you can dare to ask that he sex you rotten out loud and not feel guilty about it. That kind of attitude!

Be the Boss and Rock it Good!

You know damn well that you have power over your man and it remains in your best interest to exploit it. A visit to a sex store will leave quite an impression with the wide range of sex toys available to garner yourself. Handcuffs, neckties and scarves are goodies you can welcome aboard.

You can use these to tether his hands together in bed so he is restricted to touch you. You are probably not yet ready to up your game with real restraining, so, in this case, consider it quite okay to just hold his hands over his head.

Now let the teasing and torture begin on his naked and flamed body. While kissing your way all over his body, down to his torso, through his inner thighs and to his pelvis, makes alternative shifts back to his ears and neck, tantalizing him while he strains to touch you but cannot. While you are at it, dare to talk dirty to him.

Go an extra mile to ask how he is feeling. Allow him to describe, in detail, just how you are getting him so miserably doped with wanting you not only turns you on so bad but ignites his desires even more.

Change Positions, Find New Angles

Believe it or not, nothing screams naughty as when you explore new angles with penetration sex, especially if you choose to discover these angles from various parts of the house.

After suppressed foreplay, try bringing the action to the couch. Kneel on the cushions and have him stand up and come behind you to enter you from behind.

Breaking taboo from the norm, sex while standing communicates a fearless attitude, a daring resolution and a whole new approach to unrestricted sex. You can also choose to go an extra mile to deepen the penetration by lifting one of your legs, so that you are leaning back against his hairy chest with your foot flat on the couch.

Do a Slutty Blowjob

Maybe he is already used to getting a blowjob from you; it is likely that you are moving your mouth up and down his penis. Try using the tongue slowly winding it around his member while maintaining eye contact at the same time. Using the tip of your tongue, swirl up his shaft then while at the top, start sliding your mouth up and down in insidious motions.

While it is no secret that guys watch endless porn, to have you lick him and blow him up, just as that clip on his porn movie, becomes a dream come true.

As this becomes you bringing the house down with unimaginable shudders and contrasting ejaculations from him, you are also able to tap into some of his hidden, wildest desires.

Give your Wardrobe a Makeover

You know, taking those granny panties and old stretched shirts to bed can be a great turn off for him. The resolution: to sexy-up your wardrobe from the ground up means sexy underwear, clothes and postures too. When you wear some nice lacy thongs, this communicates to him that you are a girl who was already aware she would be getting laid later on.

Again, if you choose to shave your legs and then wear something he will need to unbuckle during sex, that says you are about to rock his world, it keeps him immensely wicked and curious, not knowing what move you will be pulling off next.

Naughty Sex Positions You Can Try

1. **Frog position** – Here, you go on top and lie with your legs and his apart as they both touch, resembling the shape of a frog as you support yourself with your hands on the bed and him pulling your hips to him.

You can try this move especially at times when you realize he is too tired to take the lead and simply allow him to lie back and enjoy the experience as you lead him on.

2. **Face to face sitting position** – In this position, you get to sit upright on his lap with both of your legs hooked over the arms of a one-sitter couch.

    Once he enters you, lean back on top of his thighs as he supports your back. On this position, he is able to kiss your breasts and also pull himself inside you in longer thrusts helping him achieve maximum pleasure.

3. **Deep penetration position-** The best thing about this position is that he is able to vary the angles at which he enters you. Lie on your back and raise your knees against your chest and your legs over his shoulders. With his knees bent, he is able to achieve the deepest penetration.

    It is not advised to try this position in late stages of pregnancy and you should also feel free to alert him when he goes too deep and it hurts. Sex should be pleasurable and not burdening.

4. **Back to front position** – In this position, he gets to lie on his back with knees raised and feet landing flat on the bed. You then sit astride him and on his penis, leaning against his knees and thighs towards his feet.

   The best thing about this position is that he can comfortably reach forward and stroke your buttocks, deriving a bewitching notch with pleasure.

5. **Advanced rear entry-** This position offers a deeper penetration and works miracles if your guy has difficulties holding his penis longer inside of you.

   Here you get to sit on his penis as he lies on his back, legs apart and with your hands firmly holding on the bed for support.

With him holding your breast area and your hair probably falling on his face, you have the mandate to ride him senseless at your own pace. Again, with his hands free to arouse you even more, there is no telling the heights of passion to be reached.

7 GET ADVENTUROUS-ADVOCATE FOR NEW THINGS

Stepping Out of your Comfort Zone

We are not advocating that you go swinging from a chandelier on him, but please find it quite okay to dirty dance for him. In essence, you will be surprised at how much pleasure you can derive and provide for your man the moment you decide to step out of your comfort zone.

While it could be just spontaneous to let your body ask for it, how about getting vocal and spell it out point-blank? Your ability to get out of a stale sex routine will have to be driven by the willingness to shakes things up a little. Did you know that it is indeed possible to have much friskier and exciting sex later on in a relationship that at the start? It all depends on whether you know what you want in bed and making a point at not being too shy to ask for it.

Sample Those Marked Territories

Well like they say: never say never! You know during your high school years when you would hear the bad girls in school narrate about how they were fucked up against the wall or had standing sex and you would try to burry your head deep with shame?

Well, that was the 'nice girl's' reaction; but today, having hit the sack countless times should already have you feeling liberated. However, mere sexual liberation is not enough; it can get boring if you keep repeating the same things every falling dawn. Bedroom monotony is a relationship killer, in fact, a great recipe for a perfect divorce.

Regardless of how well you believe your sex-life is scaling, if you don't work on revamping the energy in the bedroom, especially from your end, someone else might as well beat you to it.

Those Things you Couldn't Do?

Probably this bit will have you growling and hating on its due possibility, but well, just what if?

What if you Advocated for Anal Tonight?

Truth be told, anal is not quite an open preference with most couples often because the guy is afraid to cross the limit and the woman harbors a negative approach to the possibility. However, anal done properly can leave the 'sex of the year' impression.

The problem is that most people do it all wrong, so it hurts and it becomes a dreadful thought henceforth. Apparently, observing due patience, gentleness and a positive mindset coupled with proper clit stimulation, anal can feel as amazing as vaginal sex.

What if you Rented Some Porn?

Because most people often associate porn with guilt, it is rare to find partners who are comfortable watching porn together. However, just as the use of sex toys shouldn't be a solo-adventure, watching adult films shouldn't either.

You would be surprised at how much watching porn together can add a sizzling effect to your sex-life. It doesn't have to be brutal or animalistic but it is one thing that helps discover and explore those marked territories you never knew existed.

Often times we tend to find porn distasteful, but it actually serves as great inspiration for couples to experiment more behind closed doors. Not only is it great because it fosters a shared experience, but it also greatly helps speed up foreplay and reduce sexual fantasies.

What if you Decided to Lube it Up?

This will not be because you don't trust you can achieve the natural lubrication through foreplay; it will be because you are willing to explore other means of maximizing pleasure during sex.

Welcoming the thought of using a lubricant during sex not only enhances sensitivity but also prolongs it to garnering you and your partner's intense pleasure. Again let's face it, even with maximum foreplay, most women still fall victim of inadequate vaginal lubrication and this can really be a huge turn-off.

Inadequate lubrication leads to uncomfortable, painful sex while proper lubrication enhances rhythmic movement of both partners, respectively, and highly increasing the odds that they will climax.

What if you Delayed Gratification?

They say good things come to those who wait and this is no different when it comes to love making. Whenever you pursue instant gratification for any reason at all, that comes off outright as bad sex.

The reason why most men suffer premature ejaculation is mainly because they tend to rush orgasm, because they are lazy lovers. You know what a premature ejaculation from your man means that he is not far from 'frustration and dissatisfaction'.

Propose delaying orgasm and, if possible, direct how the sex goes to make sure that he ejaculates when the moment is just right for you both. The trick is prolonging foreplay as much as possible as this ensures that penetration only happens when the both of you are ready for the release!

8 DO'S AND DON'TS IN THE BEDROOM

Bedroom Etiquette
Apparently, there are certain approaches that if undertaken during sex or within the bedroom vicinity, become a real turn off. Again, there are those actions and deeds that are vital and that highly determine how your sex-life unfolds.

Well, don't forget that the bedroom is supposed to be the one place where you reconnect, cuddle, and get intimate. So if someone says get those gadgets out of the bedroom including the TV, then do so to give your sex-life a breather; it is vital!

The Dos and Don'ts During Sex
There is so much you can say or do during sex but then again there is so much that must be allowed to remain under the carpet. It however

seems that it is often the do's that most people overlook in the bedroom, likely because they are not aware of them. So what should the bedroom necessities consist of?

5 Key Bedroom Do's

Praise him – Praising him on his progress, making sure to let him know he is doing okay is really important. It does not necessarily have to be verbal; making appreciative noises in terms of moans or a dabbling scream when he hits your g-spot really well is sufficient also.

Communicate your needs- There is no way that you will achieve that mighty orgasm if he keeps touching all of the wrong places or doing all of the wrong moves. It is important to let him know how you wish to be touched, licked or penetrated. Let him know when a certain move makes you uncomfortable; remember: if you don't enjoy it as much, this inhibits maximum pleasure for him too.

Eye contact- This remains a crucial aspect when it comes to love making. Maintaining eye contact with your partner allows you to share in his pleasures, lets you understand how this-and-that makes him react, and, in essence, helps you know what works and what doesn't.

Facial expressions remain the most reliable

way of interjecting emotions and feelings and you can be sure to never go wrong with them.

Willingness to experiment- Sex was initially discovered on the missionary basis and that is perfect. However, sticking to one sex position can be boring and monotonous and your sex life will need some spicing up every now and then.

Tease and play along- This means playing with him and encouraging him all the same. When you feel he is really getting you there, and there is something you know he can do to garnish your orgasm, let him know. Feel free to shout "Faster" or "Harder"; he needs such inspiration to be able to bring the house down with some erotic shudders.

The Bedroom Don'ts

Some comments.. you just shouldn't make them- When he tries to go anal on you and you are uncomfortable with it, you don't use the 'hate' word. Try using less threatening and intimidating communication; this can be a mix of verbal and non-verbal with the aim of prompting him to try a different option, instead of this one; this should be done in a sensual manner.

Never fake an orgasm- Apparently, women have long been known to fake orgasms for the most selfless reasons, like trying to up their partner's ego and the most selfish ones, like trying to speed up a snoozy escapade. It is important to find your peak potential with sex because you do not deserve to miss out on the magic impact orgasms sweep onshore. You would be surprised at how willing he would be to help you get there if you would only let him know that it is taking you longer to reach orgasm and why you think it is the case.

Electronic gadgets must go- Today's economy has gotten everyone up and down, leaving close to no time for sexual exploration. Did you know that ditching your phone, iPad or laptop while in the bedroom will lead to a better sex life?

While these only serve as distractions, creating a sensual ambiance and mood- free from such distractions will help focus on your partner, their needs, and how to satisfactorily meet them.

Don't mention your ex- For no reason at all, regardless of how exceptional your ex was in bed, should you mention him, even if you are trying to hint that he tries something mind-blowing that your ex used to do.

Thinking that this will work as a challenge he will want to conquer, it might as well work as intimidation and, no man ever wants details on your previous sexual escapades. 'What he doesn't know won't kill him' is a fact that remains; the vice-versa is also quite true.

Don't beg or force things upon- If you beg for something as a tease, that is okay because it serves purpose and it is quickly over. However, when you beg for something that he is not exactly inclined to fulfill and while he might just give in, it will not be as pleasurable for either of you.

If you really love him, let him enjoy the sex and don't let your begging paint a repulsive picture in his head because if he associates this feeling with every time you are about to hit the sack, it will become a dreadful experience and not exactly fun and pleasurable.

9 FLIRTING & SEXTING IN ADVANCE

To convince a man that it is you he really wants to commit to, you surely need to rock his world in more ways than just with a great body. Just so you know, portraying a bewitching silhouette and dressing to kill won't do it if you can't actually kill 'IT' in the bedroom.

Again, sex is just a word in itself, what needs to be done before we safely arrive to that destination is focus on all of the action. So we come down to the definition of flirting. This means communicating your romantic attraction to him.

However, regardless of the platform you use to flirt, whether internet, phone messaging or face to face, it is important that you learn to balance your emotions so you can manage to both reveal your intended feelings while keeping him intrigued.

Sexting is one of the most compelling, flirtatious platforms today and is an essential tool when it comes to revamping bedroom matters.

The Power of Sexting

Sexting is ideally the exchange of dirty (sexually explicit) texts, videos or images through mobile phones. However, as sexting is a sexual art, it needs the participation of two willing partners where there is no limit on the heights of seduction that can be reached.

For women, sexting becomes the ultimate tease, with the stipulation that the guy on the receiving end really likes you back, respects you and desires to know you both intimately and emotionally. Otherwise, if you decide to sext a guy who is only after you to win a bet, sexting can easily turn out to be a miserable, electronic blowjob.

In short, making sure that the guy is deserving of the texts you plan to sext him is important and remember, also, that the idea is not to paint a bitchy picture of you but to incline a guy to surrender to the fact that you render him powerless.

So How Do You Know?

How is it that you know whether a guy is just putting you up for a prize or not? A guy who is undeserving of your participation in dirty texting is the type that makes you feel insecure in his presence and in front of his friends.

Is he emotionally distant and often runs hot and cold unbenounced to you? Without trying to burst your bubble, girl, sexting this kind of a guy is a risky move.

You will get him hooked right now with sexy mind games and talk but, considering douchebags tend to have perfected the art of pretense, there could be no winning, in this case.

How to Go About Sexting Him

Girl, it is about time that you tap into your empress personality and start telling him what it is he really wants to hear. You might have to find a way to password-protect your phone, if you know what that means.

You know best when your free times are. It could be the time spent on the bus, waiting for a flight, some free time during lunch or wherever it is that you are able to flick some keys on your phone, that end up making the desired effect, surpassing mere imaginations!

Women love reading material that makes them feel sexy and men love seeing such material that turns them on. Surprisingly, those technically inert characters on your phone have the power to heighten intimacy, bring closeness and work out the sexual chemistry between you and your man.

Try sending him something hot like "Guess what, last night is still so fresh in my mind, every touch, every caress. You should know I can't wait to see you tonight" or "Hey, can you feel my hands all up your chest? I so want to get naked with you!"

You know that hot photo you took last night while in front of the mirror with just your lingerie on? Why not just hit upload to his Whatsapp…Boom! There is all the evidence he needs to know: getting home on time will be a worthwhile attempt.

However, it is important to use intellect and know well what a woman in love or interested in a long-term relationship would say or do and how a bitchy whore would act. So yes, there is need to understand how far is too far with sexting.

10 TEN SEX SKILLS HE CANNOT RESIST

Boy, Isn't He Lucky?

You have mastered the art of locking lips with your guy for the longest time now, since you started making out back in the days. However, what most women do not realize yet is the potential their mouth carries when it comes to sexual stimulation.

Your mouth can ignite such incredible sensations in him and, like they say, great kissers make great lovers too. You know there has got to be that certain way that you kiss him that has to remind him why he is this lucky guy.

Kissing Skills you Should Try

With just your tongue, your lips and gently using your teeth, here is a combination of moves you can pull on him during foreplay.

The Ear-otic Stimulation

The ear happens to harbor some of the subtlest sensations that almost never get the chance to be stimulated. While he' would probably be experiencing these sensations for the very first time, you can bet you will blow his mind.

By placing your lips just an inch away from his ear and releasing a slow sigh, this erotically tantalizes his nerves.

There is the Roof Raiser

Sometimes while you are there, thinking you have explored every possible inch of his mouth with yours, you would be surprised to learn just how many stones still remain unturned. One area in his mouth that rarely gets the attention is the roof of his mouth, a spot that happens to be one of the most ticklish parts of his body.

So the next time you are locking lips, how about you try flicking your tongue once or twice through this spot?

The Teaser-Kiss

Often, we reason that the only way to get him curling his toes is by going for the mouth-mouth move. However, a gentle hint of a kiss serves more potently than a complete kiss would. If you focus on such delicate areas, like his face, you will be working wonders with ecstasy.

Try grazing your dry lips across his forehead, contouring slowly through and over to his temple before finally landing an actual kiss on his mouth. Simply because the dry kisses feels a lot different than the usual wet ones, the sensation brought upon induces sublime shivers sending him to a frenzy of imaginations.

A Really Handy Kiss

If you think a kiss on the hand is too innocent to use during foreplay, then you do not know anything yet. Placing the tip of your tongue at the base of his fingers, precisely on the webbed area, then gently and slowly sliding your way up the side, works incredibly to evoke sensual vibrations.

This works because this area, just like the ear, is quite sensitive and rarely gets that much attention. As icing on the cake, take the tip of his finger in between your lips; it brings goose bumps as it becomes an indirect suggestion of your mouth being down there.

The Thigh-Rise Approach

One of the most sensitive spots for a man is, no doubt, the inner thigh. From where his knee bends, plant the lightest kiss there and then work your way up while increasing the pressure your lips use on his skin as you escalate.

If you think that men do not fancy

foreplay, you are dead wrong. How about you prolong the agony by going back to where you started and do this all over again. This drives him crazy with anticipation while at the same time buying you time to get yourself ready for him.

Tango With Your Tongue

Just when he is thinking that he has felt and seen it all, prove him wrong by going a notch higher. The underside of your tongue has this silky texture that will feel sensual on most of his sensitive spots, most especially the nipple.

Since this spot is often associated with women, something only women like to be done to them, women rarely tap on the magic the spot brings and how desperately men secretly crave for attention on this spot.

Try flicking the underside of your tongue on these soft spots, side to side and then alternating with the upper, much rougher side of your tongue. This awakens his nerves and the alternating sensations keep him begging for more.

So What Happens After Sex?

After a great episode of mind-blowing, passionate sex, just a single mistake has power to spoil all the fun. Such stupid mistakes also tend to communicate that you were simply waiting for sex to be over so you could do something much more important. While these are often unintentional acts, they can end up becoming awful goof-ups that slowly kill the sexual mood.

Major After-Sex Mistakes

No man wants you participating in sex with them as a duty or obligation. In essence, if you try to get busy with something not related to the bedroom right after sex, it can make him feel disowned. It remains vital to make an effort of allowing the sexual feeling to linger on long after the act is over if you do not want to affect your sexual relationship.

Here Are 5 Common After-Sex Mistakes People Often Make:

Falling asleep right away- Rolling over and falling asleep right after passionate sex greatly kills the charm of sex. This communicates that you found it less important to reminisce on the passion you just shared, which is an important part of intimacy.

Rushing to the washroom- If you are going there to pee, that is okay but when you run to take a shower right after a magical romp, it becomes a mood spoiler. It leaves your man feeling like the sex had been unpleasing; something you could not stand after it was done.

Sleeping separately- It does not really matter whether what you just had was make-up sex because you had been fighting earlier; you simply have no sensible reason to sleep in separate rooms after a steamy lovemaking session.

While a session of intimacy is supposed to bring you two closer together, packing your sleeping details to make a shack on the couch is a killer approach. Sex rule number one, never abandon your partner in bed, ever!

Bringing the kids for a sandwich nap- It is perfectly okay to want to roll over together with the kids, but not after a steamy session of love making.

You see, after a remarkable intimate session, the sexual vibrations still linger on and who knows how far the two of you are yet to scale before morning comes.

Petty phone distractions- An emergency call or text is one thing, but calling a friend at wee hours for a petty chit-chat right after an episode of sexual pleasure? No one does that!

While it's pretty obvious that such unofficial matters can wait, getting busy on the phone or messaging makes him feel like you are not as interested as he is, therefore ruining all of the fun.

ABOUT THE AUTHOR

I am in my late 20s on the West Coast, who works for a major magazine in the United States. I love writing (whenever I get the chance) and I always want to reenact each and every part of what I write. Probably not all at once, but eventually I would love to! I mostly write erotic romances, with lots of development and of course sexy scenes!

If you have enjoyed my book, I would be eternally grateful if you would leave a review, to help other readers decide whether or not to buy my book.

Also as a side note, ALL of my titles are available in Kindle Unlimited!

Join the mailing list! You will be the first to receive news of hot new FREE or $0.99 releases as soon as they go live!
Copy and paste this link into your browser:
http://eepurl.com/bpIXqb
Thank you for your support!

Email me anything you would like me to write or would like to see more of in my upcoming books!
Veronica.summers24@gmail.com

Thanks for reading!
-Veronica, XOXO

Made in United States
Troutdale, OR
12/13/2023